TRADI VENETIAN RECIPES

Cuisine of the Serene Republic

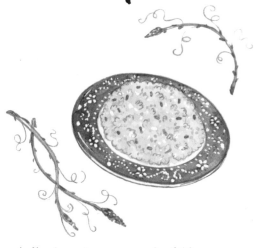

sarde'le in saòr • peoci saltài • granseo'la a'la
venessiana • fiori de suca friti • risoto nero • risoto
de bisato • papare'le coi bisi • bigo'li co' l'anara
sopa coada • tripe in brodo • figà a'la venessiana
sepe nere co'la po'lenta bianca • s'ciosi in salsa
spàresi lessi • erbete rave • fritata co'le sego'le

arsenale et editrice

CONTENTS

VENICE
AT TABLE

The special feature of Venetian cuisine is without doubt the variety of its dishes prepared using a broad range of ingredients of very different origins. Nothing could be more natural in a city that, although founded in the lagoon, always retained strong bonds with its hinterland.

Yet the "cuisine of St. Mark" is also deeply influenced by the city's role over the centuries, particularly in the period of the Serene Republic. Trade with other peoples, which ensured the impressive wealth of the city, is also reflected at table; this is why the recipes have such different identities. Mention must also be made of the influence of trade by Venetian merchants with so many different and distant countries, from the Far East to Northern Europe. Such trade carried exotic spices from Asia and the distinct taste of salt cod from the cold waters of the Baltic – but also, albeit more modestly, fish and crustaceans from the lagoon itself, fresh vegetables from the islands in the estuary and game from the hunting reserves in the lagoon. A closer look at this gastronomic experience is an ideal way to discover fascinating traditions and enjoy surprising and unexpected culinary specialities.

"Sarde'le in saòr" (sweet and sour sardines) are among the best-known dishes. Local customs actually saw every social class use different fish for the "saor" sauce but today it is made only with sardines, in keeping with the most popular tradition. Mention can also be made of "peoci saltài", "bovo'leti" and the traditional, exquisite "panada". "Figà a'la venessiana" (veal liver with onions) is one of the most typical Venetian recipes based on meat. And to finish, how can we ignore the famous Venetian desserts such as "za'leti" or the delicate "baíco'li" (delicious fine biscuits)?

Over and above these dishes, this guide includes a selection of the most emblematic dishes in the amazingly varied "cuisine of St. Mark", naturally emphasising the best–known and tastiest recipes. Enjoy your meal!

Editorial co–ordination
Arsenale Editore

Editing
Chiara Scudelotti

Photography
Archivio Arsenale

English translation
Peter Eustace

Traditional Venetian Recipes
Cuisine of the Serene Republic

First Edition January 2009

© ARSENALE EDITRICE

Arsenale Editore Srl
Via Ca' Nova Zampieri, 29
37057 – San Giovanni Lupatoto (Verona, Italy)

Hors d'oeuvres

Sarde'le in saòr
Sweet and sour sardines

*1 kg of sardines, 500 g of white onions,
3 spoons of white vinegar,
flour, extra virgin olive oil,
salt.*

Prepare the sardines by removing their heads, fins and guts. Wash well and then toss in flour.

Heat plenty of oil in a pan and then fry the sardines on both sides.

As they become ready, remove them from the pan and place on absorbent paper to dry the oil and then add salt.

Use another pan to heat a glass of oil, then add the finely chopped or sliced onions and blanche over a low flame. Then add the vinegar and simmer gently until a soft but rather dense sauce is obtained, where the onion still retains its appearance.

Place a layer of the fried sardines on the base of an earthenware pot and then cover them with the sauce. Then add another layer, covering again with the sauce, until all the sardines and "saòr" sauce are used. At the end, the fish should be covered by the marinade.

Fit a cover and leave to rest in a cool place for at least 2 days. Accompany with Bardolino or Breganze red wine.

The "saòr" sauce is a marinade based on onions. Marinating food with onion has very ancient origins in Venice (it was mentioned as early as XIV century) and was a typical sailors' dish because it helped prevent scurvy during long periods at sea.

Today, tradition has it that the Venetians prepare this dish to eat it on board boats during the night of the Redentore Festival (third Saturday of July). In any case, it is served all year round as a very tasty hors d'oeuvre.

GRANSEO'LE A'LA VENESSIANA
VENETIAN CRABS

4 medium–sized and live "grancevole" crabs,
2 lemons, 1 sprig of chopped parsley (as preferred),
extra virgin olive oil, salt, grains of pepper.

Use a small brush to clean the shells of the crabs carefully, then tie the claws to the body with kitchen string to avoid problems in the next stage.

While they are still alive, place the crabs in a large pot of boiling water with half a lemon, salt and a few grains of pepper. Leave to cook for about twenty minutes. The crabs are cooked once they turn a fine scarlet red colour. Then leave to cool in the broth. Remove, drain and cut the string. Clean the shell again to eliminate any more resistant crusts. Remove the abdominal lamina of the females, extract the eggs and place them in a bowl. Then also remove the entire underneath part of the shell and snap off the claws one by one close to the shell, taking care not to break it.

Remove the "coral" and place it in another recipient. Carefully extract also the block of pulp and dice it. Then, with the hands, separate the meat from the horny and cartilaginous parts, that should be eliminated and placed in the recipient with the coral. Use a sharp pointed utensil to complete the operation by removing the pulp also from the deepest parts. This stage also reveals the brownish, creamy parts that should be removed and placed in the bowl with the eggs. Use specific pincers or even a nut–cracker to break the claws and extract the pulp by pulling it out of the shell. Also dice this meat and add it to the other. Dress the diced pulp and coral with a pinch of salt and a marinade of pepper, lemon juice and a dash of oil. Then delicately mix all the ingredients and replace in the shells, adding a sprinkle of chopped parsley as preferred. Lastly, blend the crab eggs with the creamy parts in the bowl and serve the compost separately for diners who may wish to add it to the "grancevola" crab pulp. Accompany with Sauvignon dei Colli Berici or Soave Classico.

GRANSEO'LE A'LA
VENESSIANA

PEOCI SALTÀI
MUSSELS

1.5 kg of "peoci" (mussels), 2 cloves of garlic,
2 sprigs of chopped and whole parsley, 1 dl of oil
extra virgin olive oil, pepper, a few slices of lemon.

Remove the "beard" protruding from every mussel. Wash the mussels carefully and repeatedly in a bowl under running water, scraping them individually with a stiff brush or other utensil to eliminate every external crust.

Prepare a sauce with a sprig of parsley, 2 cloves of garlic (eliminating the green shoot inside) and a dash of oil.

Slightly oil a broad pan, add this mixture and then the mussels. Place the pan over a high flame and cover it. The mussels will be ready after some minutes (5–10, depending on quantity and size): they will have opened and produced their own salty sauce. Eventually eliminate any which are closed or empty.

Remove them from the pan using a sieved ladle and place them on the serving dish.

Filter the sauce through a strainer and then pour it over the serving dish. Sprinkle with fresh ground pepper, mix and garnish the serving dish with parsley.

Serve the mussels hot accompanied with slices of lemon, since they should be eaten one by one by using a small fork to remove them from their shells after sprinkling with a few drops of lemon juice

At the end, some diners enjoy the tasty sauce, using a shell to scoop it like a spoon or moistening pieces or bread. Accompany with Gambellara or Custoza white wine.

"Peoci" or mussels were once enjoyed in Venice harvested in the open sea, outside the lido barriers to the lagoon or, more often, from the lagoon itself and even close to St. Mark's Square.
Lagoon mussels are excellent yet almost no Venetian dares eat them raw because of pollution. Enjoy mussels by all means but always cooked and flavoured in the traditional Veneto style: garlic, parsley and pepper.

GARUSO'LI
MUREX, SEA SNAILS

*1.2 kg of garuso'li (murex, sea snails), a little lemon rind,
3 spoons of vinegar, chopped parsley and garlic
extra virgin olive oil, salt, pepper.*

Wash the "garuso'li" repeatedly in running water. Place them in a pot of cold water with the lemon rind, vinegar and a pinch of salt. Place the pot on heat and once the water begins to boil, leave to simmer for 45 minutes if young or 60 minutes if adult. Drain them and then use a toothpick to remove the meat, placing it in a bowl. As this operation progresses, also carefully eliminate the hard disks at the base of the shell that protect the softer parts.

Dress with oil, chopped parsley and garlic, salt and pepper. Accompany with Pinot Bianco dei Colli Euganei or Soave Classico white wine.

BOVO'LETI
SNAILS

*"Bovo'leti" (land snails), garlic, extra virgin olive oil,
parsley (optional), salt, pepper.*

Wash the "bovo'leti" well and repeatedly under running water. Bring a large pot of water to the boil and then add the well-washed "chioccioline". Return to the boil and leave to cook for 10 minutes. Drain and leave to dry and cool for about an hour. Serve with the sauce of oil and finely chopped garlic, adding salt and pepper as preferred. Chopped parsley may also be added by preference.

Leave the "bovo'leti" to marinate for some time and then serve cold. Best enjoyed eaten with the fingers and sucking the meat. Accompany with Bardolino Chiaretto rosé wine.

PO'LENTA E SA'LAME COTO
"POLENTA" AND COOKEDSALAME

For the "polenta" (maize flour meal): 1 kg of fine-ground yellow maize flour, 3 l of water, salt.

For the salame: 10 thick slices of home-made salame, 50 g of lard, 2 spoons of white vinegar.

Bring the salted water to the boil in a large pot, preferably in copper. Pour the yellow flour slowly into the water, at little at a time, to avoid forming lumps, stirring continuously in the same direction with a large wooden spatula. Mix frequently even during cooking; the "polenta" is ready after about an hour, when it detaches easily from the sides of the pot. Pour in to a platter and leave to set, then use a cheese wire to cut into slices of about 2 cm thick. Dice the lard and simmer it over a low flame in a broad, flat pan. When lard is ready, add the slices of salame without fully cooking them but warming on both sides. Place 2 slices of lukewarm "polenta" on each serving plate with 2 slices of cooked salame. Add 2 spoons of vinegar to the lard sauce and simmer for a minute until just warm. Then pour a little of this sauce over every plate and serve with excellent Valpolicella Classico or Merlot del Piave red wine.

FIORI DE SUCA FRITI
FRIED COURGETTE FLOWERS

12 courgette flowers, 100 g of fine flour, 1 egg, 1 glass of milk, oil for frying, salt.

Prepare a batter by beating the egg and mixing in the flour after blending it with cold milk. Pour plenty of oil into a pan and bring to boiling point. Delicately place each courgette flower in the batter, drain and then add to the pan. Turn the flowers several times as they fry. Once golden, remove with a sieved ladle and place on absorbent paper. Add salt, turn delicately and serve hot accompanied by Durello or Custoza white wine.

FIRST COURSES

BÍGO'LI CO' L'ANARA
THICK SPAGHETTI WITH DUCK SAUCE

400 g of "bígo'li" (thick spaghetti made with egg pasta),
1 young and not too large duck, removing the offal (heart,
liver and the "dure'lo" or "gizzard"), 1 onion, 2 carrots,
1 stick of celery, a sprig of sage, 50 g of butter,
50 g of grated Parmesan cheese, salt, pepper.

Scald the duck. Carefully remove the gall bladder with bile from the liver because it is very bitter. Wash the duck and the offal. Use a large pot of slightly salted cold water to boil the duck with the celery, carrots and onion. On coming to the boil, simmer for at least an hour. In the meantime, dice the offal. Gently fry the butter and sage in a pan and then delicately add the offal, as well as a ladle of hot duck broth. Add salt and pepper and simmer for 30 minutes over a low flame. When the duck is cooked, remove it and filter the stock through a fine strainer. Bring back to the boil and then add the bígo'li. When cooked, drain and turn into a hot serving pot, adding the offal sauce and sprinkling with good quality grated Parmesan cheese. The duck, in fact, is served as the second course, together with sauces for boiled meats such as green sauce or the traditional peará (pepper bread sauce) (see page 29). Accompany with Cabernet or Merlot del Montello or Colli Asolani red wine.

> **Recipe for "bígo'li" (thick spaghetti)**
> *300 g of flour, 3 eggs, salt.*
> *Prepare a "volcano" of flour on a flat surface and then add the eggs and a pinch of salt. Use a fork to blend the flour from the sides, adding a few spoons of water. Then knead the dough into a firm yet elastic mass before passing it through a pasta mill, allowing the strips to fall on to a floured surface.*

BÍGO'LI IN SALSA
THICK SPAGHETTI WITH SAUCE

*400 g of "bígo'li" (thick spaghetti made with egg pasta),
4 salted anchovies, 1 medium onion,
1 glass of extra virgin olive oil, white wine, pepper.*

Clean the anchovies and keep only the pulp. Wash well under running water to remove the excess salt and then dice. Also cut the onion into thin slices.
Use a small pot to heat the oil over a high flame and then add the onion and chopped anchovies. Before blanching the onion, interrupt cooking by adding a couple of spoons of white wine or water, lower the flame and cover. Leave to simmer, stirring occasionally, until a well-blended sauce is achieved.
Bring a pot of salted water to the boil and add the "bígo'li", separating them immediately with a large fork to prevent them sticking together. Once cooked "to the bite", toss the thick spaghetti in the pan with the anchovy sauce. Flavour with a dash of pepper, mix and serve accompanied by Garganega dei Colli Berici or Tocai Italico dei Colli Euganei white wine.

SPAGHETI A'LE VONGO'LE
SPAGHETTI WITH CLAMS

*320 g of spaghetti, 600 g of fresh clams,
400 g of peeled tomatoes, 1 dl of extra virgin olive oil,
2 cloves of garlic, 1 sprig of chopped parsley, salt, pepper.*

Leave the clams for at least 12 hours in a basin with water and salt. Change the water very frequently, adding more salt every time, until they are ready for cooking.
After this time, rinse the clams very carefully, place them in a low pan with a cover and cook until they open over a low flame. When they have all opened, remove them from the pan using a sieved ladle but keep the cooking liquid. In the meantime, bring the pot of water to cook the pasta to the

boil. Heat the oil in another pan. Add the chopped cloves of garlic, the peeled tomatoes, the filtered liquid used to cook the clams and a pinch of salt. Thicken the sauce for about thirty minutes, stirring every now and then with a wooden spoon.

In the meantime. remove the clams from their shells and only add them to the sauce once it has thickened. Flavour with chopped parsley and fresh ground pepper.

A few minutes before the sauce is ready, add the spaghetti to the boiling salted water so that they cook "to the bite" exactly when the sauce itself is ready.

Drain the spaghetti, place in serving dishes, pour over the sauce and mix delicately. Serve with Pinot Grigio di Breganze or Lison–Pramaggiore wine.

PAPARE'LE COI BISI
BROAD PASTA WITH PEAS

400 g of pappardelle, 100 g of shelled baby peas,
50 g slice of pancetta (bacon), 50 g of butter,
1 small onion, 1 ladle of hot stock, 1 teaspoon of chopped
parsley, grated Parmesan cheese, salt, pepper.

Dice the pancetta (bacon) and onion and fry with half the butter. When the onion begins to blanche, add the peas and the ladle of hot stock. Cover and simmer for 10–15 minutes, depending on the size of the peas, adding salt and pepper as preferred. When cooked, add the chopped parsley and mix.

In the meantime, bring a large pot with plenty of water to the boil over a high flame. On coming to the boil, add salt and the "papare'le", cooking them "to the bite".

Drain the pasta without completely eliminating the water, place in an earthenware pot, add the rest of the butter and then the sauce. Set off with a handful of grated Parmesan cheese, mix carefully and serve with a Soave Classico or Custoza white wine.

This classic and traditional Veneto dish is truly exquisite with the first, home–grown spring peas and home–made pasta.

"Gnocchi" are more typical of Verona than Venice – but Verona for centuries belonged to the territory of the Serene Republic. Venetian "gnocchi", made exclusively with flour, are by now uncommon. They were made before the arrival of the potato.

GNOCHI DE PATATE
POTATO "GNOCCHI" OR DUMPLINGS

For the "gnocchi": 2 kg of large, floury potatoes, 500 g of very fine, sieved flour, 2 eggs, salt.

For the sauce: 1 kg of peeled tomatoes, 1 large onion, a few basil leaves, 1 clove of garlic, grated Parmesan cheese, 1 dl of extra virgin olive oil, salt, pepper.

Wash and boil the potatoes in water for 40 minutes. Let them cool slightly, peel and mash in a large bowl. Leave to cool completely. Add the well-sieved flour, the eggs, a pinch of salt and knead until all the ingredients are perfectly blended into a soft and elastic dough.

Divide this dough into small pieces and knead one by one. Using a well-floured wooden platter, knead each piece of the dough into a roll measuring a couple of centimetres in dia-meter. Use a knife to cut smaller pieces measuring 2 cm. Then roll these pieces one at a time over the back of a fork to form grooves, pressing delicately with the thumb. Place them on a well-floured cloth ensuring that they do not touch each other, otherwise they will stick.

Fry the finely chopped onion in oil in a casserole, then add the peeled tomatoes, the chopped clove of garlic, salt and pepper. When the sauce has thickened, flavour with basil leaves, mix and take off the heat. In the meantime, use a large pot to bring plenty of salted water to the boil and then gen-tly add the "gnocchi"; as soon as the water comes back to the boil, the "gnocchi" rise to the surface. As they do so one by one, remove them using a sieved ladle and place in single serving dishes, covering each with 2 spoons of sauce. Serve with grated Parmesan cheese and Bardolino Chiaretto or Tocai Colli Berici red wine.

PASTA E FASIOI
PASTA AND BEANS

*300 g of fresh Lamon beans, 200 g of Treviso "tirache"
or another type of pasta, 100 g of pork rind or a ham
knuckle bone, 1 large onion, 1 stick of celery, 1 clove
of garlic, 1 sprig of parsley, 1 dl of extra virgin olive oil,
salt, pepper, grated Parmesan cheese.*

Chop the vegetables (excluding the parsley) and fry them in
oil in a large pot. Add the beans, 2.5 litres of water and the
pork rind. Raise the heat and leave to simmer for about 2 and
a half hours. Add salt and pepper halfway through cooking.
Remove the pork rind, cut into strips and eventually serve to
diners. Sieve half the cooked beans and pour back into the
soup. Bring back to the boil and then add the pasta, proceed-
ing until cooked. Lastly, add the chopped parsley and mix.
Serve "pasta e fasioi" in earthenware bowls, leaving to cool
somewhat, then add Parmesan cheese, pepper and oil separately. Ideal with an excellent Tocai dei Colli Berici red wine.

TRIPE IN BRODO
"TRIPPE" IN BROTH

*1.2 kg of pre-cooked beef "trippe", 50 g of diced lard,
1 large onion, 1 sprig of rosemary, 2 sage leaves, 1 bay leaf,
1.5 l of beef stock, 1/2 a glass of extra virgin olive oil, slices
of toasted bread, grated Parmesan cheese, salt, pepper.*

Blend the lard, onion, rosemary and sage in a pestle. Heat a
little of the oil in a pot over a low flame until it smokes and
then add this mixture, leaving it to fry gently for some
mi-nutes. Add the "trippe", salt, the bay leaf and cover with
water. Turn up the heat and leave to boil for a couple of
hours. If necessary, add a little hot water every now and then.
Lastly, add the boiling stock, flavour as preferred with salt and
pepper and serve the boiling hot soup in earthenware bowls
over slices of toasted bread. Accompany with grated Parmesan cheese and fresh ground pepper. This dish is ideal with
Tocai dei Colli Berici white wine.

SOPA COADA
BAKED SOUP

*3 fine young plucked pigeons, 500 g of sliced,
stale home–made bread tossed in butter, 2 l of meat stock,
1 large onion, 2 sticks of celery, 2 carrots, 150 g butter,
1/2 glass of extra virgin olive oil, 100 g of grated Parmesan
cheese, 1 glass of dry white wine, salt, pepper.*

This soup is known as "coada" (cockled) because it is baked for a long time in the oven.
Scald the pigeons and cut them into halves. Dice the celery, carrots and onion and fry gently in the oil; then add the pigeons and brown for a few minutes. Add the wine and, once it has evaporated, add the stock, salt and pepper and cover the pot. Leave to cook for half an hour. A few minutes before removing from the heat, add the cleaned livers.
Remove the pigeons from the pot and remove the bones, ta–king care not to break up the meat too much. Also remove the livers and cut in half. In the meantime, add the remaining hot stock to the pigeon sauce and leave to simmer for about ten minutes. Arrange a layer of sliced bread tossed in butter in an earthenware or glass oven dish. Sprinkle with plenty of grated Parmesan cheese and then add one–third of the pigeon meat and a little of the liver. Continue with such layers, finishing with bread. Lastly, add the stock mixed with the sauce until the dish is fully covered and place in a moderate oven (80–100 °C) for 2 and a half hours. Every now and then, add a little hot stock to keep the soup soft. When cooked, "sopa coada" resembles a thick "pasticcio" to be served with a separate cup of hot stock.
Ideal with Pinot Noir del Piave or Cabernet Riserva dei Colli Berici red wines.

SOPA DE PESSE
FISH SOUP

2 kg of assorted fish (scorfano (redfish or haddock), anguilla (eel), coda di rospo (monkfish), branzino (sea–bass), polpetti (baby octupus), calamari (squid), seppioline (baby cuttlefish), cappe sante (Cap St. Jacques)), 600 g of mussels, 3 ripe tomatoes, 2 sticks of celery, 2 carrots, 1 onion, 2 cloves of garlic, 2 bay leaves, 1/2 glass of fine vinegar, 1 dl of extra virgin olive oil, 2 l of water, a few slices of toasted bread, salt, pepper.

Clean and wash the fish, eliminating all waste (but keep the fins to prepare the stock) and cut into pieces. Chop the carrots and celery and add to a pot with 1.5 litres of water, 2 bay leaves and a little salt and pepper, add the fish fins and bring to the boil.

Smoke the oil in another large pot and add the chopped onion and cloves of garlic. Leave to thicken, then add half a glass of water, the molluscs and crustaceans (except for the mussels) and, after about ten minutes, also the other pieces of fish. Fry gently and then also add half a glass of vinegar and, once this has evaporated, the peeled and diced tomatoes. In the meantime, sieve the fish stock and then add to the fish pot. Flavour with a little pepper and bring back to the boil, simmering over a low flame for half an hour.

A few minutes before removing from the heat, add the pre–viously cleaned and purged mussels. Place a couple of slices of toasted bread in the individual serving dishes and then pour over the soup.

Accompany with Pinot Bianco Superiore di Breganze or Gambellara Superiore white wine.

PAPARE'LE COI FIGADINI
BROAD PASTA WITH CHICKEN LIVER

400 g of home–made "pappardelle", 300 g of chicken livers, 50 g of butter, 1.5–2 l of good chicken or turkey stock, grated Parmesan cheese, salt.

SOPA DE PESSE

Clean and dice the chicken livers and fry them gently in the butter; then leave to simmer with a pinch of salt.

Bring the stock to the boil in a large pot and then add the "papare'le". Cook the pasta "to the bite", drain and serve at table with the liver sauce and grated Parmesan cheese. This recipe is ideal with Bardolino Superiore red wine.

The outskirts of the territory of the Serene Republic of Venice were home to pappardelle with chicken livers – a delicate and exquisite dish "worthy of kings".

PANADA VENESSIANA
VENETIAN BREAD SOUP

400 g of stale bread, 1–1.5 l of water, 2 cloves of garlic, 2 bay leaves, 1 dl of fruity extra virgin olive oil, grated Parmesan cheese, salt.

Break the bread into pieces and place in a terracotta casserole. Add lukewarm water to this recipient, as well as the cleaned cloves of garlic, bay leaves and a pinch of salt. Leave to rest for about 10–12 minutes, then place the casserole over a low flame and simmer for about 40 minutes, stirring now and then with a wooden spoon. The mixture should become dense and creamy, without lumps. Take off the heat, blend in plenty of grated Parmesan cheese and then serve the "panada" in bowls with a dash of olive oil.

Serve with grated Parmesan cheese and fruity extra virgin olive oil for guests to add at their pleasure.

Excellent with Custoza white wine.

RISI E BISI
RICE AND PEAS

800 g of soft, young and sweet peas (including the shells) for about 250–300 g of shelled peas, 250 g of Vialone nano rice, 50 g of pancetta (bacon), 60 g of butter, 1 small onion, 1 sprig of parsley, grated Parmesan cheese, salt, pepper.

Carefully shell the peas but keep the pods and stems. Wash thoroughly. Place the shells in 2 litres of slightly salted water and boil for about an hour. Then pass the stock and the pods through a vegetable mill. This liquid will be used to cook the rice and should be kept warm. Chop the onion and pancetta (bacon) and fry with half the butter in a casserole. When the onion has blanched and the pancetta has almost dissolved, add the peas and 2 ladles of hot stock, cover and cook for 5 minutes. Then add the rice and mix, adding boiling stock and stirring until the rice is almost completely cooked. A few minutes before taking off the heat, add the chopped parsley. Take off the heat, flavour with salt and pepper, add the other half of the butter and the grated Parmesan cheese. Mix, cover and leave to rest for a couple of minutes before serving. Accompany with Durello Superiore dei Lessini white wine.

This ancient dish of the Serene Republic of Venice was prepared for the Doge on 25 April, the feast-day of St. Mark, the patron saint of the city.

RISI E SPÀRESI
RICE AND ASPARAGUS

300 g of asparagus tips, 300 g of Vialone nano rice, 1 l of stock, 1 onion, 1 sprig of chopped parsley, 1/2 glass of dry white wine, 100 g of butter, extra virgin olive oil, grated Parmesan cheese, salt, pepper.

Heat a little olive oil and 60 g of butter in a pan, add the chopped onion and blanche for a few minutes. Then add the asparagus tips and brown them slightly. Add a little salt and pepper, then the rice stirring with a wooden spoon to blend the flavours. Add the wine and, once it has evaporated, a ladle of boiling stock at a time, stirring until the rice is cooked. When cooked "to the bite", flavour with salt, add the rest of the butter, a generous handful of grated Parmesan cheese and the chopped parsley. Mix well, cover and leave to rest for a couple of minutes before serving. Accompany with Vespaiolo Superiore di Breganze wine.

RISOTO COI BRUSCANDO'LI
RICE WITH WILD HOP SHOOTS

300 g of hop shoots, 300 g of Vialone nano rice, 1 onion,
1 l of meat or vegetable stock, 60 g of butter,
1/2 glass of extra virgin olive oil, 2 sprigs of parsley,
grated Parmesan cheese, salt, pepper.

Wash and dice the "bruscando'li". Finely chop the onion and fry in a pot with the oil and half the butter; then add the "bruscando'li" and salt.. After 10 minutes, add the rice and brown while stirring for a few minutes.

Then add a ladle of boiling stock and stir; then continue adding stock and stirring until the rice is cooked.

Take the pot off the heat when the rice is cooked "to the bite" and "creamy" but dense, add the other half of the butter, grated cheese, chopped parsley, a pinch of pepper and stir to amalgamate the flavours.

Excellent with Custoza or Tocai del Piave white wine.

"Risoto coi bruscando'li" is a "poor" dish in Veneto cuisine but is even included in sophisticated and elegant menus. "Bruscando'li" are the young tips of wild hops that can be gathered in abundance in Spring along countryside ditches and overgrown land. They have a characteristic bitter and rather tart taste. Venetian market stalls usually sell "bruscando'li" in April.

RISOTO DE SUCA ZA'LA
RICE WITH SALTED PUMPKIN

300 g of Chioggia pumpkin, 300 g of Vialone nano rice,
1 l of vegetable stock, 1 onion, 50 g of butter, 1 glass of
extra virgin olive oil, grated Parmesan cheese, salt, pepper.

Carefully clean the pumpkin to eliminate the rind and the seeds, then dice or grate roughly.

Chop the onion and fry in the olive oil with half the butter, then add the pumpkin with a pinch of salt and pepper and leave to cook after adding a ladle of hot stock. Once the stock has been absorbed and the pumpkin has become soft, add the rice and stir on heat for some minutes. Then add ladles of boiling stock as required to cook the rice, while always stirring. When the rice is almost cooked, add the rest of the butter and a generous handful of grated Parmesan cheese. Mix well, eventually season with salt and pepper and leave to cook for a few more minutes until the risotto becomes "creamy".

Serve with grated Parmesan cheese separately and a fine white wine such as Pinot Bianco Superiore dei Colli Euganei.

RISOTO AL RADICIO ROSSO
RICE WITH RED CHICORY

*300 g of Vialone nano rice, 400 g of Treviso red chicory,
1 l of stock, 1 onion, 1 clove of garlic, 1/2 glass of red
wine, 50 g of butter, 1/2 glass of extra virgin olive oil,
sugar, grated Parmesan cheese, salt, pepper.*

Wash and clean the radicchio (chicory), then dice.
Chop the onion and fry with the garlic in olive oil and part of the butter. Add the diced chicory, salt and pepper and leave to cook for a few minutes, stirring with a wooden spoon. Then add the red wine (which also helps to enhance the colour of this "risotto") and evaporate.
Remove the clove of garlic and sweeten slightly with a dash of sugar.
Add the rice and flavour it by stirring delicately; then add the boiling stock a little by little as required to cook the rice,

always stirring with the wooden spoon. When almost cooked, season with salt and pepper and then cream with the rest of the butter and a handful of grated Parmesan cheese.

Serve the "risotto" when creamy and still hot, with more grated Parmesan cheese separately. Ideal with Pinot Grigio del Piave wine.

> *"Risoto al radicio rosso" is a very recent 'new entry' in Venetian gastronomy in the wake of the immense success of Treviso red chicory. This dish can also be prepared using Chioggia pink chicory or Verona red chicory.*

RISOTO NERO
BLACK RICE

*600 g of medum cuttlefish, 300 g of Vialone nano rice,
1 l of fish stock, 1 small onion,
1 clove of garlic, 1 glass of dry white wine,
30 g of butter, 1 glass of extra virgin olive oil,
salt, pepper.*

Clean the cuttlefish by removing the skin, the central bone and guts – taking care not to break the ink sac – and place all to one side.

Lastly, use a sharp knife to remove the eyes and the horny beak in the middle of the tentacles. Then clean carefully and cut into thin strips.

Chop the onion and blanche with a clove of garlic in a casserole with a dash of olive oil. When the garlic begins to brown, remove it and then add the strips of cuttlefish.

Add salt and pepper and leave to flavour for a few minutes while stirring, then add the wine and cook until it evaporates. Dilute the "ink" from the sacs in a little water and then pour into the casserole; then cook everything for about twenty minutes. Then add the rice, stir to flavour, and then add a ladle of hot stock at a time until the rice is cooked.

Lastly, season with the butter and chopped parsley and mix well. Wait a few minutes before serving, accompanied by a good Vespaiolo Superiore di Breganze or Soave Classico.

ISOTO NERO

RISOTO DE MAR
RICE WITH SEA FOOD

*1.5 kg of sea food (mussels, Cap St. Jacques and cockles),
1 kg of fish (blacktail, scorpion fish and mullet),
300 g of Vialone nano rice, 1 glass of dry white wine,
1 carrot, 1 stick of celery, 1 onion,
1 clove of garlic, 1 bay leaf, 1 sprig of parsley,
30 g of butter, 1 glass of extra virgin olive oil,
salt and pepper in grains.*

Carefully clean and wash the mussels, Cap St. Jacques and cockles. Open them in a pan over a high flame, then take off the heat and remove the meat, leaving about twenty mussels whole to garnish the dish. Strain the stock through a fine cloth and keep it for use later.

Clean the fish, eliminating the scales, heads and guts. Boil the fish in a little water with a bay leaf, a pinch of salt and a few grains of pepper. Then remove the fish, which can be enjoyed as a second course, and keep the stock.

Fry the chopped onion and the clove of garlic in the oil in a casserole; remove the garlic once it begins to brown. Add the shelled crustaceans, the wine white and, when it has evaporated, the filtered stock. Add salt and pepper. Then add the rice and flavour it by stirring for a few minutes with a wooden spoon. Then add one ladle of fish stock at a time as it is absorbed by the rice, stirring continuously.

When the rice is almost cooked, add the chopped parsley and butter. Mix well, heating for a few moments, then switch off and remove.

Place on serving dishes, garnishing with the mussels kept apart and a few whole sprigs of parsley.

This dish is ideal with a good Garganega dei Colli Berici or Vespaiolo di Breganze wines.

RISI E SCAMPI
RICE AND SCAMPI

500 g of whole scampi, 300 g of Vialone nano rice,
1/2 glass of dry white wine, 1 onion,
1 clove of garlic, 1 bay leaf, 1 glass of extra virgin olive oil,
30 g of butter, salt, pepper.

Wash the scampi and boil them for 15 minutes in 1.2 litres of water with the bay leaf and a pinch of salt. Then remove the crustaceans and strain the stock. Shell the scampi and remove the pulp, eliminating the tails.
Fry the chopped onion and the clove of garlic in the oil; remove the garlic when it begins to brown and then add the rice, stirring for a few minutes to flavour it. Add the wine and leave to evaporate, then cook the rice by adding a ladle of hot stock at a time. After 10 minutes, add the scampi meat and continue until the rice is cooked "to the bite". Blend with the butter and serve with Custoza White wine.

RISOTO DE BISATO
RICE WITH EEL

400 g of "bisato" (eel), 300 g of Vialone nano rice,
1.2 l of stock, 1 onion, 1 clove of garlic,
1 bay leaf, 1 sprig of parsley, the juice of 1/2 lemon,
1/2 glass of extra virgin olive oil,
30 g of butter, salt, pepper.

Carefully clean the eel and cut it into rings. Smoke the oil and butter in a casserole; add the chopped onion, clove of garlic and bay leaf.

When the onion has browned, add the eel rings and salt and fry gently. Add the lemon juice and half a ladle of stock and leave to cook for about twenty minutes. Then remove the eel rings from the pot and separately eliminate the skin and bones. Remove the garlic and the bay leaf. Add the rice and flavour it in the sauce by stirring delicately. The add then the eel rings and, always stirring, a ladle of hot stock at a time as it is absorbed.

When the rice is cooked, flavour with chopped parsley and a little fresh ground pepper. Mix and serve when creamy. This dish is ideal with Soave Classico Superiore white wine.

RISOTO DE RANE
RICE WITH FROGS

700 g of whole frogs, 300 g of Vialone nano rice,
1 onion, 1 sprig of parsley, 1/2 glass of dry
white wine, 1 glass of extra virgin olive oil,
30 g of butter, salt, pepper.

For the stock: 2 stock cubes, a few celery leaves,
1 small onion pricked with 2 cloves,
1 clove of garlic, 2 bay leaves, rind of 1 lemon.

Prepare a pot with 1.5 litres of water and add all the ingre-dients indicated for the stock and the cleaned, washed frogs. Bring to the boil and leave to simmer for half an hour. Once they are cooked, remove the frogs from the stock, detach the legs and throw away the rest; then remove the bones. Sieve the stock and keep it hot.

Use a casserole to blanche the chopped onion in the oil, then add the rice and flavour it by stirring with a wooden spoon. After a few minutes add the wine and allow it to evaporate. Then add a ladle of hot stock and continue to do so as it is absorbed, while always stirring. When the rice is almost cooked, add the frog meat and season with salt. When the rice is cooked "to the bite", season with the butter, chopped parsley and a little fresh-ground pepper. Blend well and serve the 'risotto' with a good Tocai dei Colli Berici white wine.

MAIN COURSES

CARNE LESSA
BOILED MEAT

1 kg of beef (rump or other cut as preferred), 1 beef knuckle
bone with marrow, 1 free–range hen (already cleaned),
500 g of calf head, 500 g of corned tongue, 1 "cotechino"
of about 500 g, 3 carrots, 3 sticks of celery with the leaves,
2 onions pricked with cloves, 2 bunches of herbs (1 sprig of
parsley, bay leaves, 1 clove of garlic), salt, pepper in grains.

Use a large pot to boil 6 litres of water with 30 g of salt to
cook the beef and hen. Add the knuckle bone, the onion, 2
carrots, 2 sticks of celery and one bunch of herbs. When the
water comes to the boil, add the beef, skim after a while,
lo–wer the heat and after an hour add the hen. Continue
skimming until the stock becomes clear. Season with grains of
pepper and leave to simmer for 2 more hours, partially covering the pot. Using 3 separate pots, boil the pricked "cotechino" for 2 hours, the corned tongue for 1 hour and the calf
head in slightly salted water with onion, carrot, celery and
flavourings for 2 hours. When all the meat is cooked, remove
from their stock and place on a serving platter, accompanied
by "perà" (pepper bread sauce). Merlot dei Colli Berici is the
suggested wine.

Recipe for "perà" (pepper bread sauce)
Excellent meat stock, grated bread, butter, extra virgin olive oil, grat-
ed Parmesan cheese, fresh ground pepper.
Butter the base of an earthenware pot, protected underneath by a
flame–pad, and pour in the boiling stock; slowly add the bread-
crumbs, stirring well until the mixture becomes soft but still rather liq-
uid. Stir in a good handful of grated Parmesan cheese and plenty of
fresh–ground pepper. Season with a little olive oil and leave to cook
over a very low flame for an hour and a half, without covering.

FIGÀ A'LA VENESSIANA
VENETIAN LIVER

*500 g of veal liver, 2 large white onions, 30 g of butter,
1/2 glass of extra virgin olive oil, salt, pepper.*

Use a sharp knife to cut the liver into thin but not too long slices. Heat the oil and butter in a pan and then add the chopped onion, cover and cook slowly (without blanching) over a very low flame, stirring every now and then.

After about fifteen minutes, take the pan off the heat and leave to cool for a while until the sauce stops sizzling.

Then add the sliced liver and return to the heat, with a higher flame. After 2–3 minutes, use a spatula to turn the slices over and cook for another couple of minutes. Turn off the heat and add salt.

Serve on heated plates, accompanying the liver with slices of toasted "polenta" or a soft, piping hot "polentina". Bardolino Superiore red wine is recommended.

PASTISSADA DE CAVÀL
HORSE STEW

*1 kg of rump or round horse meat, a few strips of lard,
1 l of Recioto Amarone, 2 small onions, 2 carrots, 2 sticks
of celery, 1 clove of garlic, 1 bay leaf, 4 cloves,
ground cinnamon, paprika, flour, 1/2 glass of extra virgin
olive oil, 30 g of butter, salt, pepper in grains.*

If you are not experienced, it is a good idea to ask your butcher to prepare the horse meat wrapped in lard.

Chop the onions, carrots, celery and garlic and place in a glass or chinaware pot. Add the cloves, a pinch of cinnamon, a pinch of salt and a few grains of pepper. Then carefully place the horse meat wrapped in lard and cover entirely with the wine. Leave to marinate for 3 days.

After marinating, remove and drain the meat, toss it in the flour and brown in oil over a high flame; then add the vegetables taken from the marinade. Once the vegetables have

FIGÀ A'LA
VENESSIANA

dried, also add the marinade liquid, cover the pot and leave to cook over a very low flame for at least 3 hours. When cooked, remove the meat and strain the sauce. Then return the juice to the heat and season with salt and pepper; then add a little butter, a pinch of paprika and a dash of flour. Leave to amalgamate and thicken, stirring with a wooden spoon.

Cut the meat into thick slices and place on serving dishes, covering with plenty of sauce. Serve with piping hot, soft yellow "polenta" accompanied by Valpolicella Classico Superiore or Recioto Amarone red wine.

ANARA CO'L PIEN
STUFFED DUCK

1 duck of about 1.2 kg already cleaned with its liver,
100 g of ground pork, 100 g of sliced bacon,
2 slices (50–60 g) of "soppressa" (or soft "salame"),
50 g of grated Parmesan cheese, 1 egg, 1 stale and grated
bread roll, 1 clove of garlic, 1 sprig of rosemary, a few sage
leaves, 1 sprig of parsley, a pinch of nutmeg, 1 glass of dry
white wine, 1/2 glass of milk, 1/2 glass of extra virgin olive
oil, 50 g of butter, salt, pepper.

Dice the "soppressa", livers, garlic, rosemary, sage and parsley; mix this mixture with the pork, breadcrumbs, milk, grated cheese, the egg, a pinch of nutmeg, salt and pepper. Blend everything with a few knobs of butter, mix well and shape into a firm rissole.

Place this rissole inside the duck and stitch the opening. Garnish the exterior with a few slices of bacon and a few sage leaves, then bind with kitchen string.

Use a baking tray to melt a little butter and oil, then gently fry the stuffed duck, turning it several times. Add the wine and then place in a pre-heated oven at 200 °C. Leave to cook for an hour and a half, basting the duck every now and then with its sauce. When cooked, remove the kitchen string and stitches, cut the duck into pieces, place in the middle of a serving dish, cover with the sauce and garnish with the stuffing cut into slices.

Serve hot with Cabernet del Piave or Merlot di Lison–Pramaggiore red wine.

LIÈVARO IN SALMÌ
JUGGED HARE

1 hare of about 1.2 kg (with liver and blood marinated separately in grappa), 80 g of bacon, 80 g of butter, 1/2 glass of extra virgin olive oil, flour, salt.

For the jugged marinade: 1 l of full–bodied red wine (Amarone della Valpolicella), 1/2 glass of vinegar, 1 onion, 1 carrot, 1 stick of celery, 1 clove of garlic, 1 sprig of rosemary, 1 sprig of thyme, 2 bay leaves, sage leaves, mint (or basil) leaves, juniper berries, 1 piece of cinnamon, a few cloves, sea salt and pepper in grains.

Cut the hare into pieces and leave them to marinade for 24 hours in the red wine mixed with vinegar, together with the chopped vegetables (onion, celery, carrot), spices and flavourings. The following day, remove and drain the pieces of hare, then toss them in a little flour. Dice the bacon and place it in a casserole with 50 g of butter and a dash of olive oil. Bring to heat and then completely brown the pieces of floured hare on all sides. As cooking proceeds, gradually add little by little some of the marinade with the vegetables and flavours until it is used up. Leave to cook slowly for at least 3 hours. In the meantime, remove the liver and blood from the grappa marinade and dice finely; then fry separately in a little olive oil with a few drops of water.

When almost cooked, remove the pieces of meat and strain the remaining sauce. Replace the sauce and meat in the pot, add the blood and liver and cook to finish.

Add salt if necessary.

Serve the jugged hare hot with piping hot "polenta" and accompany with a good Cabernet Superiore dei Colli Euganei or Pinot Noir del Piave red wine.

The tradition of "jugging" not only hare but all game is very old and today is still the most common method for preparing many meat dishes in the areas once belonging to the Serene Republic. Over the centuries, the flavours of the marinade came to include the spices imported by merchants and tastes changed in different periods. Nevertheless, wine – red or white – has always been the basic ingredient of this tasty and aromatic dish.

PORSÈ'LO AL LATE
PORK COOKED IN MILK

*800 g of pork loin, 1.2 l of milk
(or the amount in any case needed to cover all the meat),
1 l of dry white wine, 1 sprig of rosemary,
a few sage leaves, 70 g of butter, salt, pepper.*

Use an earthenware (or glass) bowl to marinate the pork meat in white wine for a couple of days. Then remove and drain the meat.

Melt the butter in a casserole and brown the meat on all sides. Add the rosemary, sage, salt and pepper. Then cover the meat with the milk and leave to simmer for a couple of hours over a low flame, partially covering the pot. Turn the meat every now and then.

When cooked, the loin must be soft and the milk reduced to a thick sauce. Cut the meat into slices, cover with the sauce and serve with Merlot del Montello or Colli Asolani red wine.

Fish main courses

Sepe nere
co'la po'lenta bianca
Black cuttlefish with white "polenta"

1 kg of medium size cuttlefish, 1 glass of dry white wine,
1/2 glass of extra virgin olive oil, 1 clove of garlic,
1 sprig of parsley, the juice of 1/2 lemon, salt, pepper.

Clean the cuttlefish, removing the skin, eyes, horny beak and guts – but keep the ink sacs separately in a bowl. Then wash them thoroughly and cut into strips using both vertical and lateral cuts.

Heat the oil in a casserole and blanche the clove of garlic; then remove it, add the cuttlefish strips and gently fry for a few minutes, stirring with a wooden spoon. Then add the wine, leave to evaporate, lower the flame, cover and allow to cook slowly.

In the meantime, break a few ink sacs into a bowl, dissolve in a little lukewarm water, strain through a cloth and add to the cuttlefish. Then simmer everything for half an hour. Add salt and pepper at the end, after tasting.

Serve the cuttlefish steamed in their black ink in the Venetian style with soft and piping hot white polenta accompanied by Vespaiolo Superiore di Breganze or Pinot Bianco dei Colli Euganei wine.

GRANSIPORI A'LA VENESSIANA
VENETIAN CRAB

4 large, very fresh crabs, fine extra virgin olive oil, 2 sprigs of parsley, 1 clove of garlic, the juice of 1 lemon, salt, pepper.

Finely chop the parsley and the clove of garlic (after remo-ving the green shoot). Carefully clean the crabs under running water while firmly brushing the shell. In the mean-time, bring a large pot of slightly salted water to the boil. Add the crabs and cook for about twenty minutes. Then remove the crabs, detach the claws near the shell and remove the lower part of the shell. Use a small fork and a nutcracker to extract the firm and creamy meat inside the shell and the claws and place in a bowl. Lastly, season with the olive oil and lemon juice, add the chopped parsley and garlic, a pinch of salt and fresh-ground white pepper. Mix well and serve the crab in its shells accompanied by a good Soave Classico Supe-riore or Sauvignon dei Colli Berici white wine.

GO IN BROETO
GOBY FISH IN BROTH

700 g of "ghiozzi" (goby fish), 1 glass of extra virgin olive oil,1 glass of vinegar and white wine mixed together, 2 cloves of garlic, salt and pepper.

Clean the fish, eliminating the guts and then wash thoroughly under running water. Use an earthenware casserole to heat the olive oil and then add the cloves of garlic without their shoots. When the garlic is browned, remove it and then arrange the fish in the pot. Add salt and pepper, the vinegar mixed with wine and just enough water to cover; partially cover with a lid and simmer for 20–30 minutes, depending on the size of the fish. Once cooked, the sauce should be rather dense and golden.
Serve the goby with slices of toasted yellow polenta. The sug-gested wine is Vespaiolo di Breganze.

CANOCIE CONSE
MANTIS SHRIMP OR SQUILL

*1 kg of very fresh mantis shrimps, very fine extra virgin
olive oil, 1 sprig of parsley, 1 lemon,
salt, pepper in grains.*

Carefully and repeatedly wash the mantis shrimps (squills).
Bring a large pot of slightly salted water to the boil with a few
grains of pepper and half a lemon.

When water comes to the boil, add the mantis shrimps and
cook for 3 minutes. Turn off the heat and leave the mantis
shrimps to soften in their own juice. Then drain them.

Shell the crustaceans, removing the heads and cutting with
small scissors along the sides of the body, the tail and underneath the head; then extract the meat and place in a bowl.

Season with a little salt, a little fresh ground pepper, lemon
juice, oil and finely chopped parsley. Mix and serve with a
chilled Prosecco di Conegliano–Valdobbiadene sparkling
white wine.

SIEVO'LI AI FERI
GRILLED MULLET

*4 mullets (250 g each), extra virgin olive oil,
lemon juice, salt and pepper.*

Clean the fish, eliminating guts, gills and scales. Then wash
in cold water and dry. Prepare a marinade with olive oil,
lemon juice, salt and pepper. Add plenty of this marinade to
the fish and then leave to savour for at least an hour in an
oval dish large enough to contain all these ingredients. Place
the grille over the hot charcoal and wait until it becomes very
hot, otherwise the fish will break when turning them.
Arrange the mullets on the grille and turn quickly once the
first side is cooked. Baste the mullets with the marinade using
a kitchen brush while they are grilled. Serve hot with lemon
quarters and accompany with Prosecco del Montello e Colli
Asolani sparkling white wine.

SFOGI AL VIN BIANCO
SOLE IN WHITE WINE

4 soles of about 250 g each, 100 g of flour,
80 g of butter, 1/2 glass of dry white wine, 1/2 lemon, salt.

Clean the soles by removing the heads and all the fins; remove the guts. Using the tip of a sharp knife and starting from the tail, cut a flap of skin, grasp it with a cloth and then rip it off quickly. Prepare the other side in the same way.

Then use the same knife to separate the fillets from the bones; rinse them quickly in lemon water, then dry and toss in flour.

Melt the butter in a pan and, when it is hot, add the floured fillets. Fry on both sides for some minutes, basting with the wine and lemon juice, and then thicken the sauce. Add salt and serve hot with a chilled Prosecco di Conegliano–Valdobbiadene sparkling white wine.

BISATO SU L'ARA
BAKED EEL

1 eel of about 1 kg, several fresh bay leaves, salt, pepper.

Rub the skin of the eel with wood ash to eliminate the fat, then cut off the head and remove the guts before cutting into pieces. Arrange the pieces of eel and bay leaves in layers in an earthenware recipient, adding salt and pepper to each layer.

Add a little water at the end and then bake in a oven at 170 °C for about one and a half hours, removing and basting the dish every now and then with the eel fat.

Serve with polenta and Tocai or Pinot Colli Berici or Colli Euganei white wine.

BACA'LÀ MANTECATO
CREAMED STOCKFISH — BACCALÀ

1 kg of wet "ragno" stockfish, very fine extra virgin olive oil, 2 sprigs of parsley, 1 clove of garlic, salt, pepper in grains.

Place the very wet stockfish in a casserole, cover with cold water and bring to the boil. Skim off and then turn off the heat, cover the pot and leave to rest for 20 minutes.

In the meantime, chop the garlic and parsley very finely. Then drain the fish, remove its skin, cut open and carefully remove all bones.

Then place the cleaned stockfish in a large bowl and use the prongs of a fork to prepare a fine pulp.

Then add a little olive oil and use a wooden spoon to beat the pulp into a cream. Always stir and beat in the same direction, adding a little olive oil as the mixture absorbs it and becomes a frothy, whitish cream. The quantity of olive oil required varies, in accordance with the more or less fatty quality of the meat.

Now add a pinch of salt, the finely chopped garlic and parsley and a dash of fresh ground pepper.

Mix carefully and serve the "baca'là" at table in a fine dish. This dish can also be enjoyed cold with slices of toasted "polenta".

Ideal with excellent and well-chilled Soave Classico or Gambellara Superiore white wine.

Salt cod made its appearance in the city of St. Mark during the late Middle Ages with the ships of Venetian merchants returning from countries in Northern Europe after their trading expeditions. "Stockfish" immediately became popular among the Venetians, who used all their imagination to invent original dishes.

Yet salt cod was especially popular in the second half of XVI century, when the Catholic Church imposed days of abstinence.

Yet recipes then became so succulent that it circumvented the precept, originating dishes utterly out of keeping with the idea of such "mortification".

RANE FRITE
FRIED FROGS

332 medium size frogs or 400 g of frog's legs,
2.5 dl of dry white wine, 300 g of flour, 2 eggs,
0.5 dl of olive oil for frying, 1 lemon, salt, pepper (optional).

Wash and dry the frogs or frog legs and leave to marinate for a few hours in the wine.
Then remove the frogs from the wine and drain, toss in beaten egg with a pinch of salt and then in flour. Slide them delicately one by one into a pan of boiling oil and fry. Once blanched and crunchy, remove them with a fork and place on absorbent kitchen paper, add a little salt and serve imme-diately with lemon quarters.
Accompany with Tocai dei Colli Berici white wine.

S'CIOSI IN SALSA
SNAILS IN SAUCE

1 kg of snails in shells but already purged,
2 glasses of dry white wine, 1/2 glass of extra virgin olive
oil, 4 cloves of garlic, 2 sprigs of parsley, 2 bay leaves,
1 bunch of celery leaves, 1 spoon of dill/fennel seeds,
salt, pepper.

Wash the snails well and repeatedly under cold running water. Fill a large pot with water and then add the snails. Bring to the boil and cook for 10 minutes, then drain the snails and place them in cold water for an hour.
Remove each snail from its shell, eliminate the swollen and blackish terminal part and disk, if present.
Chop the garlic, parsley and celery leaves. Prepare a pan with the olive oil, chopped flavourings, bay leaves, dill seeds, wine and snails. Cover and leave to simmer for 4 hours, stirring and adding a little water every now and then.
Add salt and pepper halfway through cooking. Serve with piping hot polenta and Durello Superiore dei Lessini white wine.

SIDE COURSES AND EGGS

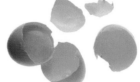

FENOCI COL LATE
FENNEL IN MILK

500 g of cleaned fennel, 30 g of butter,
extra virgin olive oil, about 3 dl of milk, salt, pepper.

Cut the cleaned fennel into halves, place in a pot, cover with slightly salted cold water and then boil for a few minutes. Drain and leave to soak slightly, then cut every piece into quarters. Melt the butter with a little olive oil in a pan and gently fry the quarters on all sides, turning as required. Cover with milk, season with salt and pepper and leave to simmer for 10–15 minutes, until the sauce becomes thicker. Serve on a dish with the sauce. Ideal with Custoza white wine.

SÈLENO RAVA
PARSNIPS

2 "sedani rapa" (parsnips), 50 g of butter,
grated Parmesan cheese, salt.

Carefully peel the parsnips, wash and cut into pieces or slices. Scald in slightly salted water until they are cooked "to the bite"; then drain. Melt the butter in a pan and brown the parsnips over a low flame. When almost cooked, sprinkle as preferred with grated Parmesan cheese and take off the heat when it has melted.
Serve with Tocai dei Colli Berici or Bardolino Chiaretto red/rosé wine.

SPÀRESI LESSI
STEAMED ASPARAGUS

1 kg of Bassano asparagus, 3 eggs, white vinegar,
extra virgin olive oil, salt, pepper.

Prepare the asparagus by cutting the stems to the same length; scrape the end with a knife from top to bottom (without touching the tips) to remove the more stringy parts. Then tie into bunches of 5–6 asparagus.

Place them in slightly salted cold water using a specific, tall pot so that the tips protrude from the water. Cover and boil for 20–30 minutes, depending on dimensions.

In the meantime, prepare a sauce of boiled eggs roughly chopped with a fork; then are a little salt and pepper, and a dash of white vinegar and olive oil; then blend all these ingredients. Remove the asparagus from the boiling water when ready, cut the strings and arrange on a serving dish with the tips facing inwards. Then sprinkle with the sauce pre-viously prepared and serve with Pinot Grigio di Breganze or Pinot Grigio del Piave.

ERBETE RAVE
BEETROOT WITH HERBS

4 medium size beetroot, extra virgin olive oil,
a dash of vinegar, salt, pepper.

Clean the soil from the beetroot and soak them in fresh water for about an hour; then cook with the skin in slightly salted boiling water. When they become soft, drain and leave to cool. Peel the boiled beetroot, cut into thin slices and dress with olive oil, vinegar, salt and fresh ground pepper. This dish can also be enjoyed cold as a side course for "frittate" (omlettes), boiled eggs or mixed boiled meat.

Excellent with Valpolicella Classico red wine.

PISSACANI O ROSO'LINE IN TECIA
TOSSED DANDELION OR POPPY SHOOTS

800 g of dandelion or poppy shoots, 100 g of lard,
extra virgin olive oil, 2 cloves of garlic, salt, pepper.

Clean and prepare these vegetables by eliminating the outer leaves but keeping and scraping the roots. Then wash carefully several times in cold water.

Then place them n a large pot of slightly salted water, bring to the boil and leave to cook for half an hour. Drain and allow to cool a little. In the meantime, dice the lard and then fry in a pan with a little olive oil with whole but peeled cloves of garlic. Then add the boiled vegetables and a dash of pepper and leave to season on heat for about twenty minutes, stirring every now and then. Add salt if necessary.

When cooked, remove the cloves of garlic and serve as a side course for mixed boiled meat and roasts. Accompany with Valpolicella Classico or Cabernet del Piave red wine.

FRITATA CO'LE SEGO'LE
OMELETTE WITH ONIONS

8 eggs, 2 onions, 60 g of butter, salt, pepper.

Beat the eggs in a bowl with a little salt and fresh-ground pepper. Cut the onion into thin rings and blanche (but not brown) in a pan with the butter.

Then pour the scrambled eggs over the onions and mix. Once the omelette begins to firm on one side, shake the pan to detach it and use a large lid to turn it over to cook the other side. Serve the "frittata" or omelette hot on a round dish accompanied by Tocai dei Colli Euganei white wine.

Desserts

Baíco'li
Baícoli

400 g of fine flour, 60 g of fine sugar,
70 g of butter, 1.5 glasses of fresh milk,
1 egg white, 15 g of beer yeast,
salt.

Dissolve the yeast in half a glass of lukewarm milk. Heap 100 g of flour on a pastry board, dish the top and add the milk and yeast. Knead into a rather firm dough (add a little more flour if necessary). use a knife to cut a cross on the top and then place the dough in a bowl, cover and leave to rise for half an hour in a lukewarm place.

Then sprinkle the remaining flour over the pastry board with the sugar, butter at ambient temperature, whipped egg white and a pinch of salt.

Knead this mixture with a little lukewarm milk as required to prepare a dough resembling bread; split into 4 parts and then roll out into pieces 4-5 cm long.

Place them on a buttered oven tray well separated from each other so that there is enough space for them to rise for the second time and then bake. Leave to rise again for about an hour and a half. Then place in the oven at 180 °C and bake for about 10 minutes, so that the dough colours without crusting or browning.

Lastly, leave the biscuits to cool and then rest wrapped in a cloth for a couple of days. Now use a sharp knife to cut them into thin, irregular slices before slightly biscuiting them in a hot oven.

These delicious biscuits can be served with coffee or "zabaione" and keep for a long time in a well-closed tin box or glass container. They are ideal with Recioto di Soave dessert wine.

ZA'LETI
YELLOW BISCUITS

250 g of fine maize (corn) flour, 250 g of fine flour,
200 g of butter, 150 g of sugar, 100 g of raisins/sultanas,
4 eggs, milk, grated rind of 1 lemon, vanilla flavouring,
icing sugar, salt.

The name of these typical Venetians biscuits was inspired by the yellow colour of the maize–corn flour, they are also known as "gialletti". They were once a speciality of the Carnival period but are now available in Venetian pastry shops all year round.

Wash the raisins/sultanas and leave them to soften in a little water; in the meantime, beat the eggs with the sugar in a bowl. Mix the two types of flour in another bowl, add a pinch of salt, a dash of vanilla and the grated rind of a lemon.

Then mix the two flours, the beaten eggs, knobs of butter at room temperature and the drained raisins/sultanas dried with a cloth.

Knead this mixture, adding a little milk if necessary to soften. Roll out to a diameter of about 6 cm and then cuts into pieces of 7–8 cm, shaping them into small ovals.

Butter an oven tray, arrange the ovals on it and bake at 180 °C for about 20 minutes (cooking time may vary depending on the size of the "biscuits").

When baked, remove the "za'leti" from the oven, sprinkle with icing sugar and leave to cool before serving with chilled Custoza or Vespaiolo di Breganze white wine.

All our books are produced entirely in Italy using papers from specifically dedicated forestry operations with regular replanting.
Moreover, all materials used are ecology–compatible in full respect of the environment and people.
All our production is based on full respect of regulations concerning safety, consumer health and our workers.

Printed in January 2009
by EBS Editoriale Bortolazzi-Stei
San Giovanni Lupatoto (Verona)
Italy